ANIMAL BEHAVIOR

JOSEPH MIDTHUN   SAMUEL HITI

BUILDING
BLOCKS

SCIENCE

WORLD
BOOK

www.worldbook.com

World Book, Inc.
180 North LaSalle Street
Suite 900
Chicago, Illinois 60601
USA

For information about other World Book publications,
visit our website at www.worldbook.com
or call 1-800-WORLDBK (967-5325).
For information about sales to schools and libraries,
call 1-800-975-3250 (United States),
or 1-800-837-5365 (Canada).

Building Blocks of Science:
  Animal Behavior
ISBN: 978-0-7166-7876-2 (trade, hc.)
ISBN: 978-0-7166-7884-7 (pbk.)
ISBN: 978-0-7166-2959-7 (e-book, EPUB3)

Acknowledgments:
Created by Samuel Hiti and Joseph Midthun
Art by Samuel Hiti
Text by Joseph Midthun
Special thanks to Syril McNally

TABLE OF CONTENTS

There is a glossary on page 30. Terms defined in the glossary are in type **that looks like this** on their first appearance.

WHAT IS BEHAVIOR?

Any action an animal makes...

...or any response to change in its environment, is called a behavior.

All animals have **behaviors**.

In fact, animals know many things from the moment they are born.

This type of behavior is called **instinct**.

Instincts are inherited (passed down) knowledge that helps an animal to survive on its own.

Some animals also learn new behaviors as they grow.

These are called **learned behaviors.**

HOP.

Humans are animals, too!

You use both instinct and learned behaviors to survive.

Behaviors in many **organisms** are instinctive.

Instinctive behaviors are not learned but are decided by the genetic makeup of the organism.

Wipe wipe wipe

Most organisms have thousands of **genes** with many possible combinations.

DNA

If you pay close attention to an animal's behavior, you can see that some animals know to do some things without being taught.

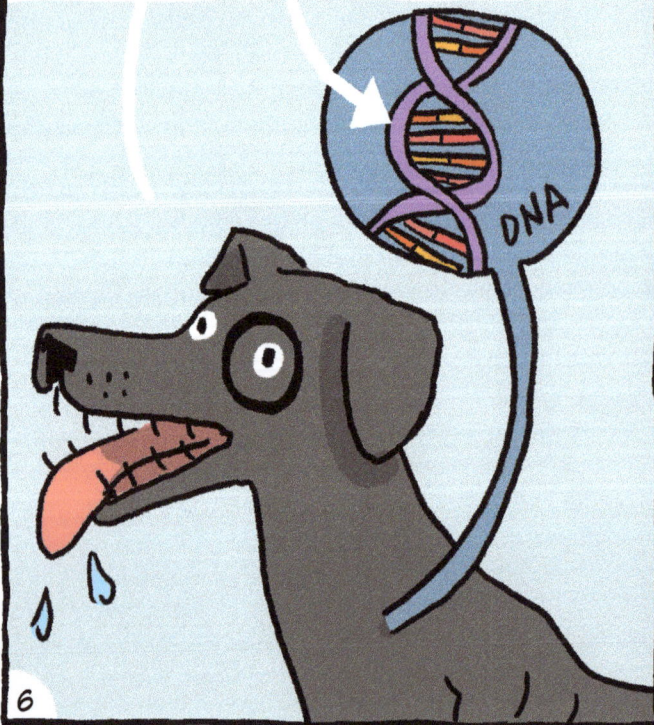

yum yum yum

FIDO

It's important to note the difference between instincts and **reflexes**.

A reflex involves some **stimulus** that causes a response.

BARK
BARK
BARK

Shivering is a reflex.

Many warm-blooded animals' bodies are triggered to shiver when they grow cold.

Even you!

When you shiver, your body is adjusting your temperature without being told.

scratch
scratch
scratch

7

INSTINCT AND SURVIVAL

Instincts may also be triggered, or stimulated, by something in an animal's surroundings.

But, not all instincts need a trigger.

A spider isn't triggered to build its web— it is just part of being a spider.

Instincts are particular to a certain kind of animal.

Animals usually cannot resist their instincts, and instincts are not easily changed.

Bzzz

This helps to make sure that an animal knows all of the behaviors it needs to survive.

OOF!

If its web gets knocked down, this spider could not catch prey.

BZZZ

Because of its instinct...

...it won't starve.

Instead, it will rebuild its web!

Mice instinctively avoid areas that smell like cats.

Sniff Sniff

They avoid these areas even if they have never even seen a cat!

Squeak

Zoom

No one teaches mice to fear cats.

This instinctive fear helps mice avoid being eaten.

LEARNED BEHAVIORS

All animals are guided by instincts.

But animals vary in how much they rely on instincts and how many new behaviors they can learn.

Learning is a process where behavior develops and changes within environments.

Insects and spiders are driven by instincts for almost all their behaviors.

In other words, they have very little ability to learn.

Amphibians, fish, and reptiles may learn some behaviors.

But most of their behaviors are guided by instincts, too.

Birds and **mammals** have instincts, yet they can still learn many new behaviors.

That's right! That's right!

Human beings, like you, can learn the most of all.

HOP

HOW ANIMALS LEARN

Some animals learn by watching.

A learned behavior comes from an animal's experience. Older animals teach young animals learned behaviors.

Some animals learn by playing.

Usually, one or both of the parents teach the young.

Animals must be intelligent to learn behaviors.

Many animals teach their young to find food and avoid danger.

crunch
crunch
crunch

Chimps like to eat termites.

But, termites live in places that chimpanzees can't reach!

Chimpanzees can capture termites by pushing twigs into termite mounds.

This is not an instinct!

Young chimps must learn how to use the tool.

Similarly, some monkeys make a loud sound to warn others of a dangerous eagle.

OO-OO-WAH!

They use another sound to warn of a nearby tiger.

In order to understand where the danger is coming from, young monkeys need to learn these different sounds.

COMMUNICATION

Some animals learn behaviors as a way to **communicate** with one another.

Dolphins may communicate with one another using a complex series of whistles and clicks called phonations.

The animals make these sounds in air-filled sacs...

...connected to their blowholes.

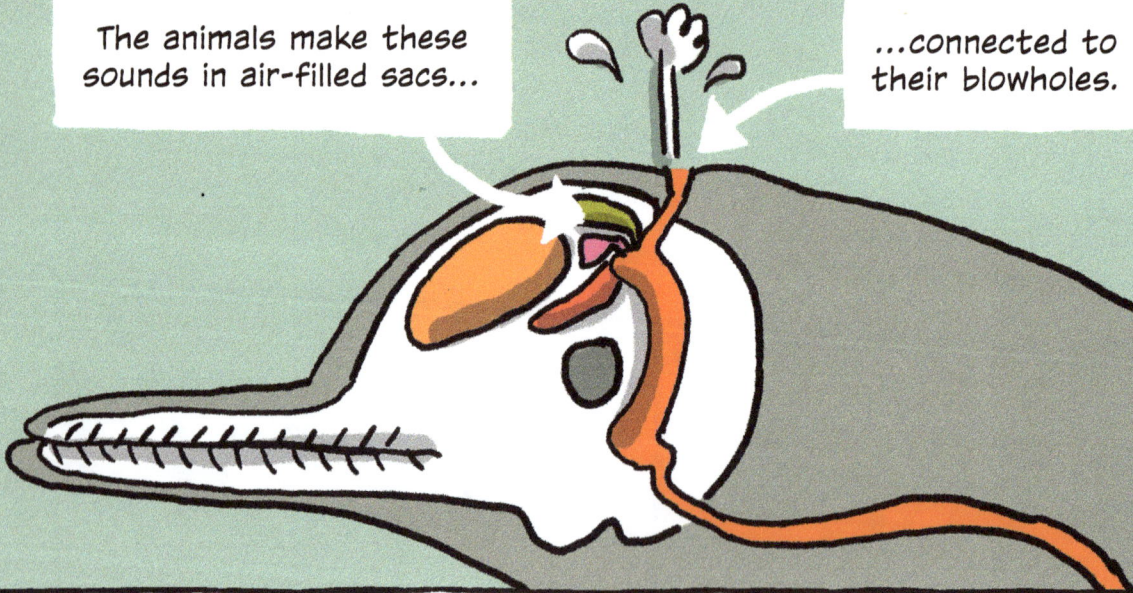

Dolphins also communicate by slapping their flukes on the water surface.

Birds use learned vocal behaviors, such as calls and songs, to communicate with one another.

KAW! CA-KAW!

Birds communicate almost entirely by sounds in habitats where they may have trouble seeing one another.

WATCH IT!

CA–

Social insects, like ants, bees, and termites, communicate with one another using sound, touch, and scent.

Honeybees use a dance to tell other members of the hive the direction and distance to a food supply.

tap tap tap tap

Hey!

Over here!

GROUP BEHAVIOR

Many animals live in groups for a variety of reasons and learn behaviors from other members of the group.

Groups help animals raise and watch over their young.

Group members can also learn how to play and to defend themselves, and learn about safe living spaces.

Living in a group also helps animals to find food and recognize which foods are safe to eat.

Peck Peck

Many animals live in groups for protection from **predators**, or hunting animals.

But, some predators also hunt in groups.

Bawk

Bawk

Bawk

By working together, the predators can tire out larger **prey,** such as moose.

Lions live in social groups called prides.

Some pride members hunt together and sometimes set traps for prey.

For example, a lion may hide in tall grass near an antelope.

SHH.

Another lion then charges from the other side.

SURPRISE!

WHAM!

When the antelope flees, it runs into the trap set by the hidden lions.

Birds in a flock can take turns watching for danger.

Splash

Schools of fish sometimes form swirling underwater spheres made up of hundreds of fish.

Predators like sharks have a hard time catching a single fish from the swirling sphere.

Orcas can also hunt with members of their social group, called a pod.

Working together, a group of orcas can separate a seal from its other group members.

The pod can also team up to catch and eat larger prey, like a young gray whale.

Many animals have instincts to seek shelter to survive.

The behavior of building a home also provides protection from predators.

Meerkats dig burrows.

dig
dig
dig

Some birds build their nests out of twigs or grass.

These nests provide a safe place for the birds to raise their chicks.

POP

crack

What's cracking?!

Beavers build large shelters in the water.

Beaver lodges are made from trees the beavers cut down with their teeth.

They also use the same materials to build beaver dams.

Beavers can really change their surroundings.

TIMBER!

WUMP

The dam floods the river and creates a lake-sized moat around their house.

21

Some instincts are triggered by outside changes.

If they need to, animals of all kinds will travel extreme distances to find food, create **offspring**, or avoid harsh weather.

This behavior is called **migration**.

Honk
Honk
Honk
Honk

MOVERS

MOVERS

Migration is when an animal travels to a new area that offers better living conditions.

Many birds migrate.

The Canada goose flies to northern Canada in the spring.

It lays eggs and raises chicks there.

As the weather turns cold in the fall, the Canada goose flies south to Mexico.

One of the largest migrations takes place in eastern Africa.

More than a million wildebeest, thousands of gazelles, and many zebras migrate when their food supply runs low.

These animals must cross rivers filled with hungry crocodiles.

But the reward of finding food and water aplenty is worth the risks of migration.

Snap

HIBERNATION

Other animals survive harsh conditions through a behavior called **hibernation.**

Hibernation is an inactive, sleeplike state.

A hibernating animal has a lower body temperature than normal.

The animal's breathing and heartbeat slow down.

Many bears enter a kind of hibernation.

Hibernating animals need little food to survive.

This allows animals to live through winters when food is hard to find.

Z.

Most animals hibernate underground.

ZZZ.

When warm weather returns, hibernating animals wake up.

YAWN!

stretch

They are often thin and very hungry after many inactive months.

Many small mammals, such as bats and ground squirrels, hibernate.

Lizards, snakes, and other reptiles can also enter a state like hibernation.

Hmm.

AMPHIBIAN HIBERNATION

Unlike mammals and birds, reptiles and amphibians are **cold-blooded**.

Most amphibians, like frogs, have moist skin.

If their skin dries out, they will die.

HOP

In hot, dry areas, most amphibians avoid the sun and are active at night.

Plop

In some climates, there are times when even the nights are too dry for amphibians to survive.

Gulp.

So, amphibians in these areas must enter into another kind of hibernation.

They store up as much water as they can...

Slurp.

...then, they dig burrows and go into a deep sleep while they wait out the dry season.

When moisture reaches their underground burrow, the amphibian becomes active again and digs its way back to the surface.

POP

Areas with harsh winters pose another difficult challenge.

HOP

To survive the seasonal changes, amphibians in these areas dig burrows under logs, or even at the bottom of ponds.

As the temperature drops, a special substance in the amphibian's body allows it to freeze solid without being harmed.

The amphibian remains frozen through the winter.

As spring arrives and the ground temperature rises, the amphibian slowly thaws.

drip drip

Then, it returns to the surface, ready to face another summer!

BOING

27

ANIMAL BEHAVIOR

Around the world, examples of animal behavior can be witnessed both day and night.

By moving together as a herd, most of these animals are protected from predators.

This helps when animals travel long distances or migrate to find food or water.

But, when a sick animal is separated from the group—

—it doesn't stand a chance.

The lions work together to hunt.

These predators are **nocturnal.**

They are often active at night.

Hyenas also work together, but to scavenge from the lion's kill.

A hyena's mouth waters as a reflex to the smell of meat.

Whether learned or instinctive, any action an animal makes, or any response to change in its environment, is a behavior.

You are able to learn new behaviors, but you also have instincts.

Hah Hah Hah

And, just like other animals, how you respond to your environment can affect everything else around you, too!

GLOSSARY

behavior any action an animal makes in response to its environment.

cold-blooded animals whose body temperature changes to match the temperature outside.

communicate actions, sounds, and smells that animals use to share information.

genes a part within a cell that controls an organism's traits.

hibernation an inactive, sleeplike state that some animals enter in the winter or dry season.

instinct (instinctive behavior) behaviors, or actions, that animals know from birth, without needing to learn from experience.

learned behavior any behavior, or action, that an animal must learn through experience.

migration the movement of groups of animals to new locations with better living conditions.

mammal a class of animals that has a backbone, grows hair, and feeds its young on the mother's milk.

nocturnal a living thing that is active at night instead of day.

offspring the young of an organism.

organism any living thing.

predator an animal that hunts and feeds on other animals.

prey an animal that is hunted by other animals for food.

reflex an automatic body response to a stimulus.

stimulus something that causes a reflex, or response, in the body.

FIND OUT MORE

Books

The Animal Book: A Visual Encyclopedia of Life on Earth
by David Burnie
(DK Publishing, 2013)

Animal Encyclopedia: 2,500 Animals with Photos, Maps, and More!
by Dr. Lucy Spelman
(National Geographic, 2012)

Bird Talk: What Birds Are Saying and Why
by Lita Judge
(Roaring Brook, 2012)

Elephant Talk: The Surprising Science of Elephant Communication
by Ann Downer
(Twenty-First Century Books, 2011)

How Animals Work
by David Burnie
(DK Publishing, 2010)

Super Nature Encyclopedia
by Derek Harvey
(DK Publishing, 2012)

Wild World: An Encyclopedia of Animals
by Jinny Johnson
(Millbrook, 2013)

Websites

BBC Nature: Animal and Plant Adaptations and Behaviours
http://www.bbc.co.uk/nature /adaptations
Ten animal behavioral patterns are examined in short units, complete with topic introductions and wildlife video examples.

McGraw Hill – Virtual Lab: Mealworm Behavior
http://www.mhhe.com/biosci/genbio /virtual_labs_2K8/labs/BL_18/index.html
Take a peek inside the behavior of a mealworm in this clickable virtual lab with bonus comprehension questions.

National Geographic Kids: Creature Features
http://kids.nationalgeographic.com/kids /animals/creaturefeature/
Select an animal to watch a video or hear its call, or read an article to learn more about its unique characteristics.

National Geographic Kids – Reptiles: Baby Chameleons
http://video.nationalgeographic.com/video /kids/animals-pets-kids/reptiles-kids /chameleon-babies-kids/
Listen to a narrated video describing how instinctive behaviors help baby chameleons hatch from their shells!

PBS – Nature: Animal Behavior
http://www.pbs.org/wnet/nature/category /episodes/by-topic/animal-behavior/
Learn about some of your favorite animals while watching videos about their wild behaviors!

San Diego Zoo Kids: Games
http://kids.sandiegozoo.org/games/
Meet your favorite zoo animals through a variety of activities include drawing, games, and crafts.

Scholastic Teachers: Science Study Jams!
http://studyjams.scholastic.com /studyjams/jams/science/index.htm
All of your questions about plant and animal life will be answered in clickable lessons featuring narrated slideshows, key terms, and short quizzes.

INDEX

www.ingramcontent.com/pod-product-compliance
Lightning Source LLC
LaVergne TN
LVHW070840080426
835513LV00023B/2415